Bobby the Bunny Learns all about Money
© Jake Swan 2024

Illustrations © Jack Bateman, used by permission
jackwbateman@gmail.com

Layout and editing by Galleon Publishing
editor@gallleonbooks.ca

Mayhem Books
Saint John, New Brunswick, Canada

ISBᵘN 978-1-998122-04-2

MAYHEM
BOOKS

BOBBY THE BUNNY

LEARNS ALL ABOUT MONEY

JAKE SWAN

On the far edge of town, there stood a small house;

So tiny it might have been built for a mouse.

But while mice well did come, and mice well did go,

This house was not built for the mice! Heavens no!

A family of bunnies, instead, lived inside—
This one-bedroom shack, ten feet long, eight feet wide.

The father was Richard, the mother was Lynn,
And the kids were Lucinda, and Phoenix and Gwynn,

And Dexter, and Kevin, and Cal, Brent and Squee,
And Chrissy, and Jack, Brian and Johnny-Lee,

And Peter, and John, and one-eyed Cousin Rob—

But the youngest and sweetest of bunnies was Bob.

Needless to say, they had nothing flash;

They were real rich in love, but were sure poor in cash.

Lynn taught French 101 at the local high school,

And Richard repaired the mill's large paper spools.

They did honest work, and they went at it hard,

And thus managed to keep carrot plants in the yard.

Carotte

But one summer night, when Bob couldn't sleep,
He heard his dad all choked up, trying hard not to weep.

"What will we do, Lynn, when it starts to snow?
When wintertime comes? When the icy winds blow?

We've got nothing stored! I just can't seem to save!
Will our sweet little home be our tiny mass-grave?"

Bob covered his ears, shook the words from his mind,

But thoughtful was Bobby, and caring and kind.

So to solve all their woes, he was racking his brain,

When the solution hit home with the force of a train!

He inherently knew of a single great truth:

A rodent could always spare one little tooth!

He tied one end of floss to his left front incisor,

And the other end to their Corolla's sun visor.

Richard started the car and took off to the mill,

While Bob clung to a tree-trunk with all of his will.

The string tightened fast; the incisor went "Pop!"

The world went grey and fuzzy, then Bob's body went "Plop!"

The plan, he supposed, must have had several flaws.

He came back to the world in his big brother's paws.

"You lucky rabbit!" Peter wearily said.

"You lost a front tooth, but at least not your head!"

"What now?" asked Bob quickly; "What thing do I do?

To attract what's-her-name? To bring in you-know-who?"

"The fairy?" Peter asked. He was simply astounded.

"Has anyone told you you aren't very grounded?"

Peter explained what Bob needed to know.

Bob prayed that the lady would leave him some dough.

He awoke with the sun, and he screamed, with a thrill,

"The tooth fairy left me a five-dollar bill!"

"You lucky rodent!" his siblings all said—
"What will you buy with your Tooth Fairy bread?"

"Candy!" "No! Chocolate!" "No! Stuff for PlayStation!"
But Bob's only goal was preventing starvation.

That evening his dad drove him out to the store,

To buy whatever thing Baby Bob could afford.

He carried back wood scraps and nails to the car,

And learned in the process five bucks won't go far.

But Bob worked through the night on his top-secret plan,

And the next day revealed— a Carrot Juice Stand!

"By the side of the road, with rush hour both ways,

I'll sell carrots and juice to commuters each day!"

After one week, when he counted his money,

It had doubled to ten! He was no stupid bunny.

Peter seemed jealous, so Bob took him aside,

"I can teach you to work, and to build up your pride!"

So back to the store, they bought one more load,
And now they had stands on both sides of the road.

Soon they had fifty-five dollars in hand!
The brothers were proud! These bunnies felt grand!

"Peter there's something I think you must learn,"
Bob said, before laying out all his concerns.

But Peter was confident, "We've salvaged the day!
We made fifty-five bucks, Bobby! Hip-Hip-Hooray!"

They presented their earnings to Richard that night,
But their dad only sighed, and his smile went tight.

"Boys, how I'm proud of you! Boys, how you've grown!
Boys how you've reaped all the seeds that you've sown!

"But I'm terribly sorry, it's with great hesitation,
That I must teach you guys about hyper-inflation.

See, when government spends so they get re-elected,
They leave bunnies like us out of luck, unprotected!"

"Back in 2015, boys, this would have been plenty!

In fact, we'd get through a bad winter on twenty!"

"But with CPI climbing, and no end in sight,
We'll be lucky if fifty-five buys us one night!"

The news wasn't hopeful, their future looked grim;
It seemed they were trapped by the Central Bank's whim!

But while Peter despaired, Bobby thrust out his chin:
"Tell us how do we do it, Dad? How can we win?"

"The math," Richard said, "calls for a strategy switch."
But he hung his head low: "If I knew, we'd be rich."

Bob hit the library, and read all he could find,

About equities, T-bills, distributions-in-kind.

He learned ledgers and assets, debt instruments too;

He learned margin, and yield, S&P, QQQ.

But the greatest of all, though he seemed kind of gruff,

Was a guru of money, named Warren the Buff!

Warren warned to invest couldn't guarantee gain,

And that amateur hopes often ended in pain.

"Don't buy in high spirits, don't sell when you're tearful,
When others are greedy, smart bunnies are fearful."

But Warren said there was a chance not to fail,
Though the bears of the world had the bulls by the tail.

"Right now they're terrified, selling it all!
So man-up," Warren said, "show them that you've got gall!"

Bobby and Peter waved their family goodbye;

It was off to a broker, it was make good or die!

On the way to the bank, by an old fast-food dumpster,

They were stopped by a rabbit, their dad's friend, Mr. Dunster.

"Boys!" he cried merrily, "is that cash in your hand?

I can help you get rich, if you follow my plan!"

Bobby wanted to run, but Peter said, "Just a sec.
Maybe his way is faster. Hear him out. What the heck?"

"Boys, have you heard of the magic of memes?
Where valuation is made of fantastical dreams?

If you lend me that money, I'll give a thousand-fold back!
You won't be counting your bills, you'll be counting your stacks!

"I'll buy crypto, and Coinbase, and Doge, GME!
I'll buy Research in Motion, and more AMC!"

"To be honest," Bob said, "that's a fool's speculation,
And dumpsters aren't known for top-notch sanitation."

The surly old rabbit waved them off with a flip,
And mumbled to himself about "Buying the dip."

The brothers decided they'd stick to their plan.
If they'd had proper fingers, they would've shook hands.

The broker was friendly, it was obvious why—
He'd get paid if they lived, and get paid if they died.

Bob knew there'd be costs. To invest isn't free.
He bought a fractional share of Berkshire Hathaway – B.

It was a rough go at first, as the markets went down,

And he worried their share would end up in the ground.

But he kept it invested, and by selling more juice,

He bought share after share, while he hoped for a boost.

When the market recovered, and it finally did,

They'd made enough for the winter, and a few extra quid.

And now Bobby's a hero of family renown,

And his broker's the richest dang rabbit in town.

THE END